так...

0.0

⋮

0.0

⋮

DEDICATION

For my family and friends.
Special shoutout to Allan Espiritu.

0.0

⋮

0.0

⋮

AUTHOR'S NOTE

Hey there! My name's Hyun. I live in New York City and I'm a designer at IBM Research. More importantly, I'm fascinated by all things Eastern Europe—the history, the culture, and the architecture. I also enjoy experiencing the region through pop culture. I've sunk countless hours into *S.T.A.L.K.E.R.*, one of my favorite video games and one of the most popular modern depictions of The Exclusion Zone. Though I'd never been to Chernobyl before this trip, I had an emotional connection to its sights and sounds thanks to this game. And yes, I read too. I own a copy of *Roadside Picnic*, the famous Russian-Soviet science fiction novel by Arkady and Boris Strugatsky.

The Chernobyl disaster is emblematic of how technology can backfire and how developments made with good intentions can cause widespread harm. Consequently, I believe everyone has a responsibility to be vigilant witnesses of technology in order to ensure something like that never happens again. We need to understand and respect the forces we are trying to tame with scientific breakthroughs. Nuclear power is a fearsome example.

In short: we only have one planet, so let's not try to blow it up, all right?

INTRODUCTION

People keep asking me why I went to Ukraine. I wish there was some grand story to tell, but I just decided to go one morning while at work. My usual reply to the question starts with "so…", and I figured this was the perfect title for this book. "так" can be used as "so…" or "hmm…" in Russian. I had always wanted to visit Eastern Europe, and I knew a bit of Russian, so I chose Ukraine. As soon as I had plane tickets in hand, I knew I needed to visit Chernobyl.

We have seen the pictures of the distant and impersonal catastrophe before, but I wanted to know what normal life there had been like before the accident. I wanted to know what kinds of stoves families used to cook dinner. I wanted to know what books were stacked on their night stands. There's more to the exclusion zone than the disaster itself.

For the moments I couldn't capture, I asked my mom, a painter, to recreate them. These images are my input filtered through her artistic lens. As I roamed the zone, I also found beautiful typography, artwork, and designs in general. I asked a friend to reinterpret a portion of the artwork through digital illustration. For typography and packaging, I took a stab at recreating them digitally. I didn't want to take anything out of the zone, as that's not safe, and is certainly not respectful. The recreations in this book are my way of preserving what I found without disturbing the places I visited.

Finally, a disclaimer. This book isn't meant for historical, political, or technical reference. Those topics have been covered extensively in great works you can find online. This is just a humble record of my trip to Chernobyl, written down and distributed in hopes of teaching somebody something new.

I can't think of a better way to get started than with the immortal words of Yuri Gagarin, the first man in space, said just before launch: *Поехали*! ("Let's go!" / Pie-Ah-Khali!)

Hyun

CONTEXT

Don't worry, I'm not going to bore you with a long history lesson about the Chernobyl accident. However, I think some background information will help put my photos in context. If you already know about the disaster or just want to see my pretty pictures, skip ahead. If you want a deeper dive into nuclear engineering, read Wikipedia.

Here's what you need to know. The Chernobyl Nuclear Power Plant, situated outside of Pripyat in Ukraine, blew up in the early hours of April 26th, 1986. There's nothing particularly juicy about it. No terrorists. No big mushroom cloud like in the movies. During a late-night test, a power surge hit the plant. The workers tried to shut the reactor down, but it was too late. Too much steam had built up and eventually caused a lethal explosion. This exposed the core's graphite to oxygen, and a massive fire broke out.

40-second shifts.

All the while, radioactive material was billowing into the sky thanks to the plumes of smoke. A 10-kilometer exclusion zone ("the zone" from here on out) was established soon after. This was a smart move; 49,000 people were living in Pripyat at the time. As you'll see in my photos, they had to evacuate quickly—and they were told they'd only be gone for three days. Much was left behind, which is why Pripyat looks like it's frozen in time. Eventually, the town of Chernobyl had to evacuate as the zone was increased to 30 kilometers.

A widespread cleanup effort followed. Entire villages were razed to the ground and buried. Reactor no. 4 was covered by a hulking steel structure meant to contain the radiation long term. This replaced the original covering, which had been referred to by the morbidly accurate colloquialism "the sarcophagus." The liquidators had to fight for recognition and health benefits. Hundreds of thousands of people were permanently displaced.

The accident shocked the world. Backlash against nuclear power swept the globe. To this day, Chernobyl is still synonymous with nuclear disaster. An entire Ukrainian generation lost their belongings, homes, or even their lives. The zone is now a ghost of its former self. The wind whistles through long-abandoned plazas, grocery stores, and schools. Contrary to pop culture, and public opinion, the zone is not a barren wasteland. People still live within the forbidden boundaries. Some are authorized, such as government workers, while others simply refused to leave their homes when the evacuation orders came.

The goal of the book is to turn this bleak story into an optimistic one. Yes, there is still life in the zone. Yes, there is still beauty in the zone. Read on and see for yourself.

VISITOR'S CENTER

I wore my Sekonda watch during my trip. The brand was made in the USSR and later sold by a British company. I thought it would enjoy a trip back to the old country, even if it might not have specifically come from Ukraine. The boots that carried me through Chernobyl were originally purchased for a hike in the Catskills. Yeah, they were just as surprised to be there as I was.

MY WATCH AND BOOTS

Here's the entrance sign for the Chernobyl Nuclear Power Plant, ground zero for the meltdown. See that pipe in the lower left corner? I guess it's meant to pump water somewhere, but I remember asking myself: who maintains it? Even in Chernobyl, of all places, some regular person is laying pipes and upkeeping them. I was beginning to realize there was a new life here. The disaster had destroyed an old city and birthed a new one.

CHERNOBYL NUCLEAR POWER PLANT SIGN

MY TRIP ANSWERED OLD QUESTIONS AND RAISED NEW ONES.

One of the first creatures I met in the the zone were
these friendly pooches. The official stance of the
State Emergency Service of Ukraine is "no petting
allowed," but how could any dog owner resist these
cuties? Believe it or not, the dogs were quite happy.
They got snacks and much coveted under-the-chin
scratches. Pretty good deal if you ask me. Of course,
there's no way to be sure how they were affected
by radiation, but they looked healthy enough.

There's an interesting relationship between the
dogs and the people who live and work in the zone.
Some of them try to examine, medicate, and tag
the dogs for tracking purposes. Others just name
the pooches and feed them as if they're family
pets. Sadly, it still isn't an easy life for these cuties.
Someone told me a litter of pups had been born
six weeks before my trip, and only two survived.

One last thing: I met a special dog named Tarzan
in a very special place. I'll talk about him later.

This newspaper dated March, 1986 shows a "road-map" to the year 2000 for the communist party. Kinda presumptuous, don't you think? The Soviet government constantly looked ahead without addressing problems in the present, and we all know how that turned out. Anyway, *слава*! (Glory!)

WHETTING THE APPETITE

This is from a Lada, a common Russian car brand.
This car wasn't much more than a metal skeleton—
even the B-pillars had been cut from the chassis.
I guess some stalker (a person who explores
the zone) was trying to make the first-ever Lada
convertible. I mean, who wouldn't want to put
the top down and feel that Chernobyl air rush
through their hair?

THE DISASTER
HAD DESTROYED
AN OLD CITY
AND BIRTHED A
NEW ONE.

An eerily quiet road farther into Chernobyl.
What struck me the most was how similar it
was to places I'd seen in the United States.
This photo easily could've been taken in a
Pennsylvania suburb except it was taken in
a radioactive disaster site. One of the biggest
surprises was how ordinary the scenery was
in such an extraordinary place. The only
thing missing was the smoke coming out
of the chimneys.

Nowhere to go but forward.

WHETTING THE APPETITE

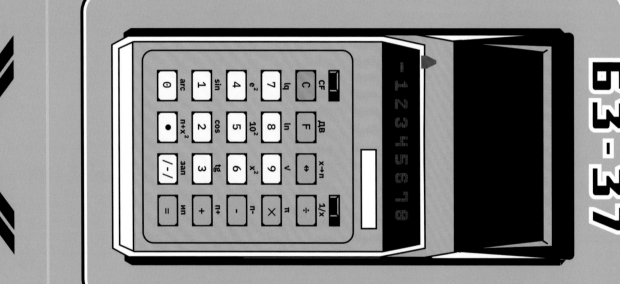

МИКРО КАЛЬКУЛЯТОР

ЭЛЕКТРОНИКА Б3-37

ЭЛЕКТРОНИКА Б3-37

THERE WAS A SIMPLE AND DANGEROUS SOLUTION.

51°25'49.94", 30°18'87.33"

WHETTING THE APPETITE

ANYWAY,
слава!
(GLORY!)

...

WHETTING THE APPETITE

Not too far from the entrance sign, there was a visitor's area for people like me. It had a small market, an office building (surprisingly occupied), and a museum that I was told was never open. There were also newly-erected statues and others that had been rescued from inner parts of the zone. This visitor's area was the only functioning settlement in the zone, and I had to go through a checkpoint here to venture any farther in. I took my time to make sure I was ready since there would be no going back until the day was over.

Pictured is a "memorial." The signs looked like those you would see while entering or leaving any Eastern European city or town, and the area looked relatively normal at first. Then, it dawned on me— these were all of the Ukrainian and Belarusian towns affected by the disaster, and these signs were like headstones in a graveyard. I'd already known the disaster had far-reaching consequences across many borders, but it hadn't felt real until now.

Usually, town signs are wrapped up in happy memories for me. Remember being stuck in a car for hours and hours on roadtrips? Remember the excitement of passing a sign with your destination on it? These used to be familiar landmarks for people. These used to give joy to homesick travelers and restless tourists. Now, the only people who pass the signs are visiting the zone, a place where even happy memories are haunted by the nuclear specter.

You've got mail! This is a Soviet-style mailbox. Speaking of, did you know you can still send letters to Chernobyl?

ПОЧТА

I FOUND TRACES OF LIFE.

Fun fact: this is the last statue of Lenin in Ukraine. After the country went through decommunization in 2015, symbols like this were outlawed. It was left standing since the statue was rarely seen by the general public.

This church was right next to the visitor's area. It is the only open church in the zone. The gardens were meticulously trimmed, and they looked like they belonged at a luxury hotel. As you'll see, the church was the most colorful building in the zone. It was the first of many hidden pockets of beauty I stumbled upon.

IT LOOKS ALMOST NORMAL, RIGHT?

Before moving deeper into the zone, I spotted a random guy ice fishing. Sounds like the set up to a joke, I know, but it's daily life for these hard-working people. Apparently, there are giant catfish in the river. Don't get too excited—they aren't mutated video game monsters. The fish just don't have many predators, and the workers constantly feed them.

FISHING

CHECKPOINT

51°29'86.03", 30°18'70.00" – 51°30'54.58", 30°06'98.91"

Here it is, the point of no return. I was near the power plant when I had to stop at this checkpoint. In fact, I had to pass through several of these in the zone. Guards inspected every inch of every vehicle for radioactive material. Can't be too careful, I guess. The bus in the photo was transporting workers into the zone. And you think your job sucks?

Earlier that morning, I saw a solitary man standing alone in the dark at an old bus stop nearby. He might've walked miles from his home just to wait for a long bus ride to start. There was a train for the workers too, since most are too poor to own cars. Even if you did have a car, would you want to drive it in the zone? I already hear enough people complain about the road salt in the northeast US. Imagine what radioactive material would do to the resale value of your pre-owned Honda.

As you can see, the workers looked like regular folks (because they were). I'm still not sure what most of them actually did, though. I only ever saw them shoot the shit and smoke cheap cigarettes. The people doing the tough jobs were probably in places where tourists would never find them.

I heard there are currently about 3,000 people living and working in the zone. Most obviously, some maintain the massive structure covering reactor No. 4 to prevent more radiation from spreading. It's popularly known as "the sarcophagus." There are also people who manage the civil infrastructure—the facilities that provide food, electricity, heat, and water to the inhabitants. When westerners think of Chernobyl, they don't realize there are normal people making a living here. I met firefighters, cops, and other civil servants. This isn't some lawless wasteland. In fact, there are even stop signs written in English instead of Cyrillic script. I doubt anybody would give you a ticket for a rolling stop, though. Let me know if you ever get a moving violation in Chernobyl.

MOVING FARTHER INTO THE ZONE

After I made it through the checkpoint and got closer to the power plant, I passed through the small town of Kopachi. The place had very few buildings left because it was the site of a special experiment. The Chernobyl liquidators (military and civil personnel who cleaned up after the meltdown) demolished and buried Kopachi's buildings to test if that was an effective way to contain radioactive material. Sadly, the experiment started and ended in this town. Traveling to each town, surveying for radiation, demolishing the buildings, and burying them just wasn't cost-effective.

It wasn't all a waste, however. Since the buildings in Kopachi had mostly been wood, which absorbs much more radiation than concrete or brick, it was much safer for the town to be buried than left standing. The Red Forest is an infamous example of what happens to irradiated wood. The affected pine trees in it were a deeply unnatural shade of ginger after they died. Like Kopachi, the only solution was to bury parts of the forest.

Aside from buried buildings, there wasn't much else to Kopachi except this World War Two memorial (or Great Patriotic War as it's known in Post-Soviet states). Statues like these are common throughout the country since many Ukrainians fought in the war.

That's me! I visited one of the government offices just outside of Chernobyl for lunch. The name was so catchy I can barely remember it: Їдальня ЧАЕС №19 ("Dining Chernobyl No 19"). Visitors to the facility must go through a radiation check as shown in the picture. The interior of the building was sterile like a hospital, complete with muted colors, stainless steel furniture, and people in scrubs. Despite Chernobyl's reputation for being contaminated and dirty, the building was probably cleaner than your kitchen.

As I walked through the halls to the cafeteria, I passed a vacation calendar for the all-female kitchen staff. Like the seemingly normal road earlier, this mundane object took on new meaning because of where I was. It's hard to believe people living in Chernobyl still worry about ordinary things like work shifts and vacation days. In Chernobyl, anything you'd normally disregard instead incited endless questions. Where did these women live? What did they do on their time off? Did they have to take care of families in this place?

Pictured is some of the best food I've ever had. No joke. The food itself was fine—hell, anything would've tasted good after walking five hours in the zone—but where I was and why I was there helped the experience become more than the sum of its parts. We were served the typical sweet and sour salads, bread, cabbage soup, rice with onions and carrots, pork with peppers and onions, and apple blintzes topped with sweet *smetana* (sour cream). The meal also came with pear and apple kompots, a sweet drink made by cooking fruit in water and sugar. Damn, I'm getting hungry just thinking about it.

The cafeteria was filled with sounds of silverware clinking and people chatting. It was surreal. I hadn't been expecting any domestic warmth in a place synonymous with radiation and destruction. I remember one conversation in the cafeteria very clearly. A guy told me what we were all eating had been a typical Soviet meal, and then he smiled. Like he was seeing something he'd thought he'd never see again.

I also learned this food related fun fact in that cafeteria: *"blin"* and *"blyat"* are sometimes used in the same way the English-speaking world uses "fudge" and "f**k." So, if little Anatoli is eating dinner with his family and spills hot borscht on his lap, he would yell, *"ay bly—"* then smoothly transition into, *"ay bly-innnnn."*

Isn't that fudging cool?

DUGA-1

51°30'56.45", 30°07'39.72" – 51°27'38.34", 30°21'98.75"

IS IT SOME SENSE OF OWNERSHIP OR STEWARDSHIP?

It might look like a creepy abandoned building, but this was just somebody's office back in the day. I mean, the IBM Research lab I work in is cool, but it's not "I work in a radar facility that could detect a nuclear bomb before it hits my country" cool. The following pictures were taken in and around this structure.

Next Page

I'm still not sure what these circuit boards were for, but I found them in a room filled with endless rows of empty frames that looked like mainframe or supercomputer racks. Was it for blockchain? Deep learning? Quantum computing?

These controls were part of a simulator most likely used to train Duga operators. The buttons in this photo were lit by a gigantic fusion reactor floating in the sky, A.K.A the sun.

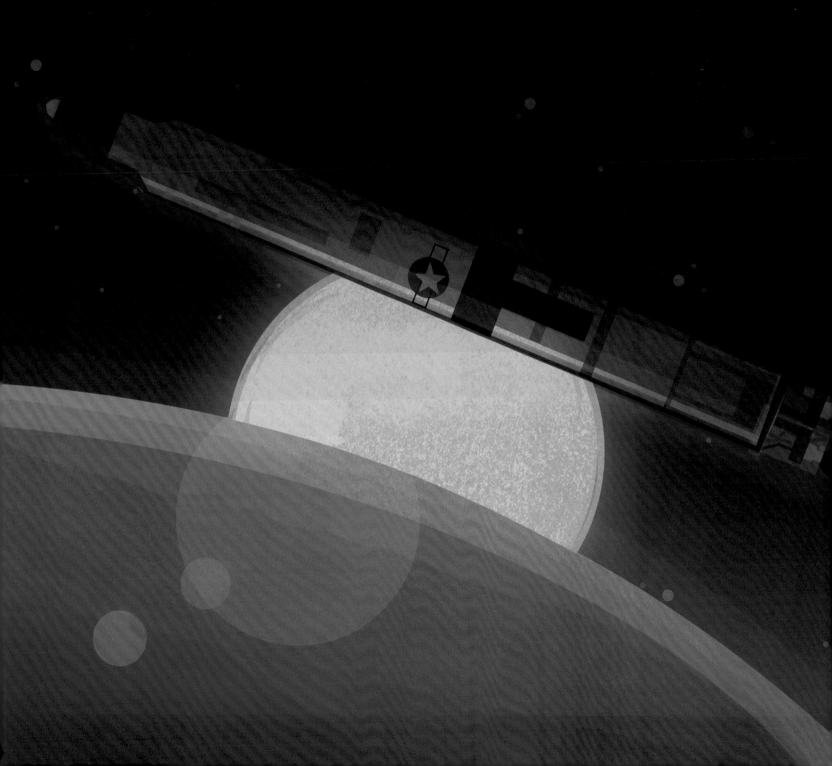

WE GET NUMB TO IT.

These control covers were manufactured by hand. If you look closely, you can see a grid drawn on with approximate center marks for drilling. I personally think the Soviets should have consulted Dieter Rams on the design.

Next Page
No Librarians in sight, and I couldn't find Artyom either. Maybe next time? I think this was some sort of server room, but I'm not sure. Perhaps they were simulating the trajectory of missiles that had gone ballistic? I bet a cheap Casio watch has more computing power than whatever had been in this room.

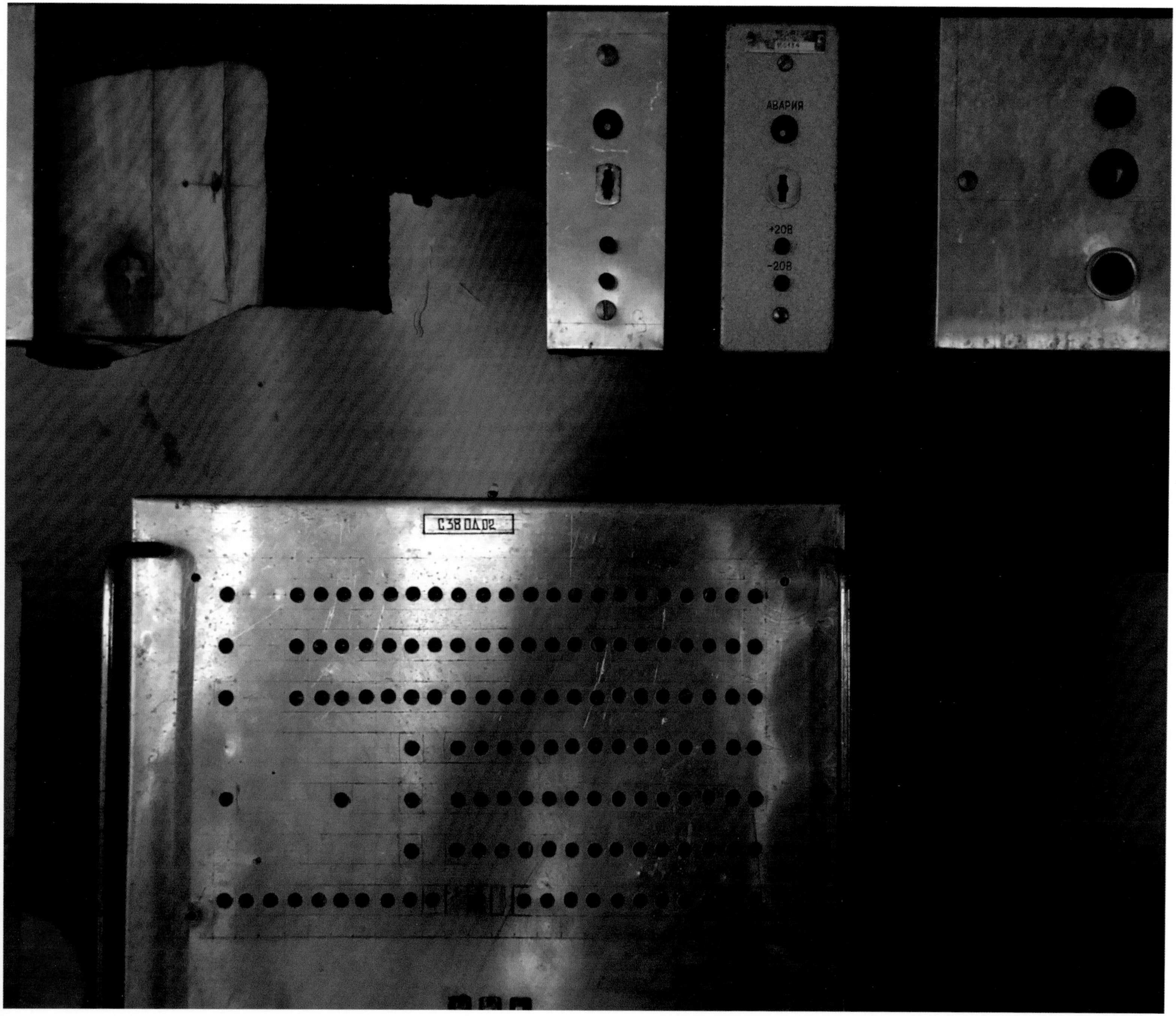

SIMULATION / TRAINING ROOM

51°30'54.58", 30°06'98.91"

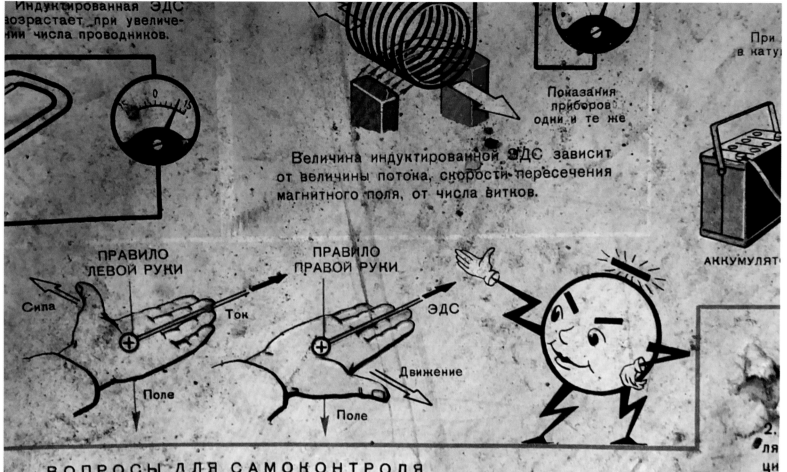

Индуктированная ЭДС возрастает при увеличении числа проводников.

Показания приборов одни и те же

Величина индуктированной ЭДС зависит от величины потока, скорости пересечения магнитного поля, от числа витков.

аккумулят

ПРАВИЛО ЛЕВОЙ РУКИ

Сила — Ток — Поле

ПРАВИЛО ПРАВОЙ РУКИ

ЭДС — Движение — Поле

ВОПРОСЫ ДЛЯ САМОКОНТРОЛЯ

...ий вокруг магнита направ-
...юсы притягиваются в том
...притягивает гвоздь вслед-
...ндукция наводит полюсы...
...чник помещен в магнитное
...0 силовых линий, пронизы-
...равен магнитной индукции...
...ик имеет магнитную индук-
...нению с 10 Гс в воздухе.
...ть этого феррита... 8. Ток
...ез катушку с 25 витками,

линии. Если скорость пересечения возрастает, то...
12. В проводнике, проходящем перпендикулярно плоскости листа, ток протекает сверху вниз. Проводник имеет магнитное поле, направленное...
13. При наличии двух магнитных полей поле сильнее там, где магнитные силовые линии... 14. Соленоид представляет собой катушку, которая действует, как стержневой магнит, при... 15. По катушке, состоящей из 80 витков, протекает ток, равный 100 мА. Определите число ампер-витков. Если число витков увеличить до 100, какой необходим ток...

ОРУЖИЕ МАССОВОГО ПОРА

К ОРУЖИЮ МАССОВОГО ПОРАЖЕНИЯ ОТНОСИТСЯ ЯДЕРНОЕ И

Ядерным оружием называют оружие, поражающее действие которого основано на использовании энергии, освобождающейся при ядерном взрыве.

3 м

0,7 м

Вес 4100 кг

3,25 м

1,5 м

Вес 4500 кг

Американские атомные бомбы «Малыш» и «Толстяк», сброшенные в 1945 г. на японские города Хиросима и Нагасаки,

поражающему и разрушающему действию ядерный взрыв в тысячи раз превосходит самых крупных фугасных бомб.

I'M STILL TRYING TO ANSWER THIS MYSELF.

SIMULATION / TRAINING ROOM

Here's the big daddy, the Duga-1 receiver. To give you a sense of scale, each of those silver, conical drivers is the size of a pickup truck. I was told modern phones have better receivers than this entire array. Think about that the next time you want to complain about your crappy cell service.

Most people familiar with the area think the Chernobyl power plant was built to supply energy to this monstrosity. There's a town that was built around the receiver just to house the radio's military staff. The town had everything you'd expect in a normal one except it was hidden from the public. People who wanted to communicate with the town had to send letters to a fake address. Then, the post office workers would recognize the "address" and reroute the mail to the secret town.

Want to know how to get into the town? Easy. Just use the fake bus stop. No, seriously. The bus stop to get there was decorated with murals of children and the government claimed the stop was for a local athletic training facility. In reality, there was no such facility. The bus stop led into the secret military town that was made for personnel running the radar array.

Sadly, the people living in this military town weren't allowed to leave when disaster struck because they were assigned to assist with the cleanup. Conversely, people in the nearby city of Pripyat were evacuated a day after the accident. They were told by authorities to pack essentials only as they would be able to return in three days. The scary part is, announcements of radioactive fallout and its effects were never broadcast from any authority. The evacuees were oblivious. I bet even the local town police didn't know of the radioactive danger.

I was told any important documents had been spirited away to Moscow after the accident. Even today, the Ukrainian government doesn't know exactly what the military was doing in this area. This is typical. Bigger countries have taken advantage of Ukraine throughout history.

Even though the receiver mostly survived the disaster, people are worried it's going to collapse soon. The force of the fall would spread radioactive particles everywhere as it slammed into the ground. Even worse, it could disturb the reactors.

DUGA ITSELF

THIS WAS WHERE
I MET TARZAN,
THE BEST GOOD BOY
IN THE ZONE.
HE FOLLOWED ME
AROUND LIKE HE WAS
MY PROTECTOR AND
LED ME TO TRAILS.

Detail of those conical structures I mentioned earlier.
Remember each one is the size of a car.

After visiting the Duga, I returned to Chernobyl
to spend the night.

Pictured is a nearby memorial. It's dedicated to the
liquidators who sacrificed their bodies to contain
the radiation. It was built from the same concrete
as the original sarcophagus.

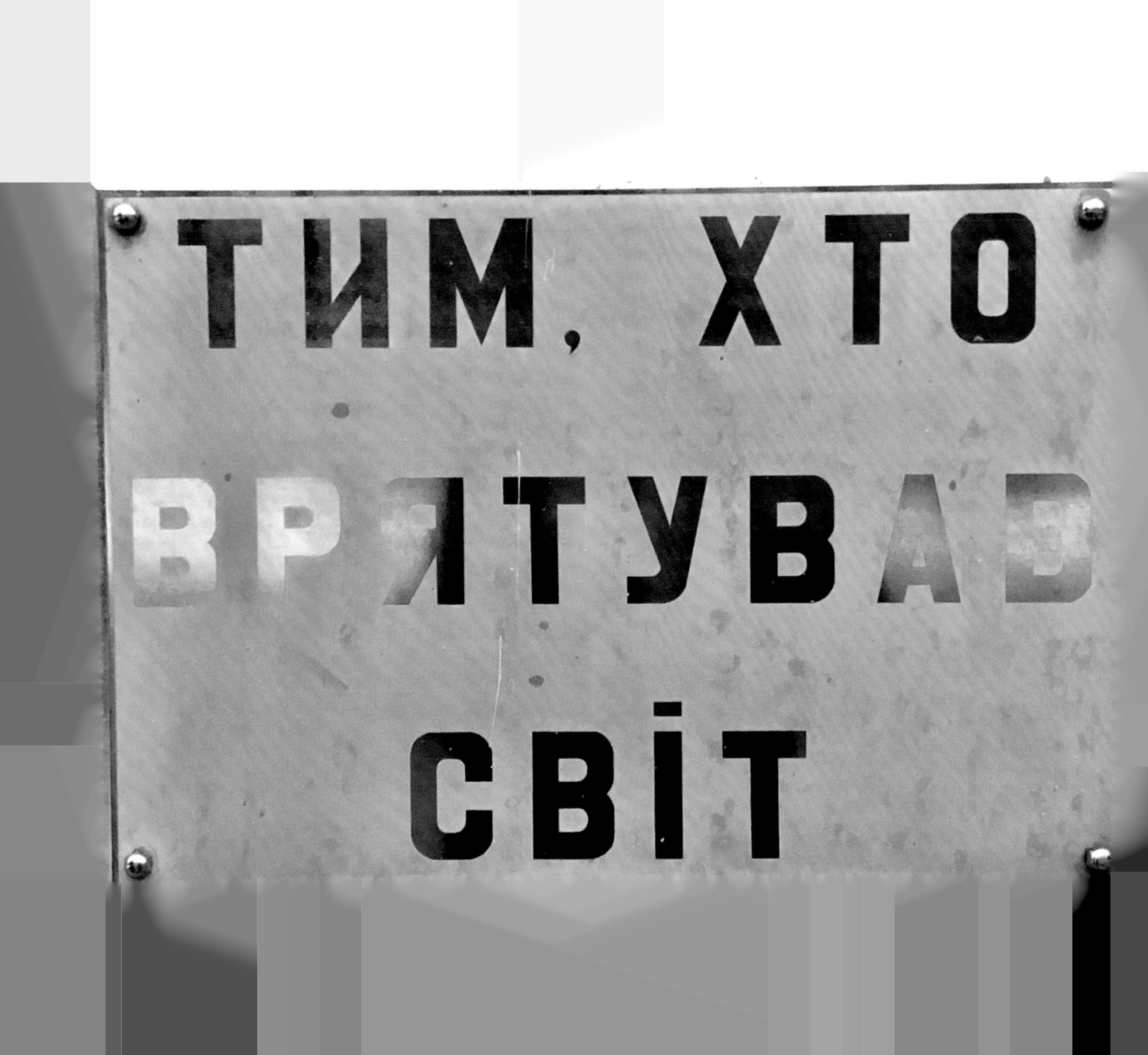
ТИМ, ХТО
ВРЯТУВАВ
СВІТ

"TO THOSE WHO SAVED THE WORLD."

It wasn't Wawa, but it did just fine. This tiny store sold everything a wanderer like me might've needed. When I walked in, I asked if anybody had seen Sidorovich. The only answers I got were odd stares. My favorite part of this mom and pop shop was the ancient tube TV behind the counter. I felt like I'd went back in time.

If you're a fan of *S.T.A.L.K.E.R.* like me, you may recognize this store. Doesn't it look like the bar area? It's possible the developers visited here during their research. Even though I'd never physically been to this place, I felt a connection. I was living a scene out of my favorite video game.

Since the shop didn't have any kvass, a fermented drink made from rye bread, I bought a 2-liter of some good ol' fashioned cola. I also picked up a bag of sushki, a mildly sweet cracker like a small, dried bagel. The lady who owned the store convinced me to buy Chernobyl fridge magnets as a souvenir. Shoot me an email if you want me to mail you one.

After visiting the store, I went to the hostel I'd be sleeping in. There were four or five of these hostels available to the general public. Long-term residences were open to workers and government officials. Unfortunately, I didn't take any pictures of my room. It was pretty much a motel with a shared bathroom.

A small café was attached. It had TV, wireless internet, bathrooms, fresh towels, and wild dogs barking up a storm outside. Honestly, I didn't need anything else —well, except bottled water. Despite the warm hospitality, I was still waiting for somebody to yell, "I said come in! Don't stand there!"

The weirdest part of the hostel was how I had no complaints. It was totally fine. By the way, the hostel had the best internet connection out of anywhere I visited in Ukraine. How the hell does that work? Maybe the Radiation™ boosted the signal.
Suck it, Verizon.

ЧОРНОБИЛЬ
ЧАЕС
26.04.1986

РАДИАЦИОННАЯ ОПАСНОСТЬ

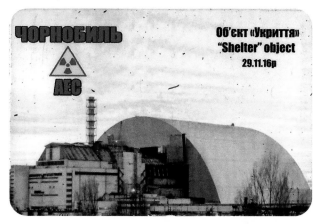

ЧОРНОБИЛЬ
АЕС

Об'єкт «Укриття»
"Shelter" object
29.11.16р

ЧОРНОБИЛЬ

1986   2016

ЧОРНОБИЛЬ

If you've never had sushki, it tastes like aerated animal crackers covered in poppy seeds. It's similar to Japanese kanpan or hardtack. The cola tasted like it had actual spices in it.

Next Page

For dinner, the café served me a glass of berry kompot, some kind of makeshift pizza, and an Uzbek pork and vegetable rice dish called plov. It tasted OK. Honestly, I preferred the government meal. For breakfast, the café served pan-roasted chicken and mashed potatoes with coffee and, you guessed it, kompot. I was jealous of the people eating eggs at the next table over, but I don't think the customer is always right at Chernobyl Café.

I recreated the breakfast I had in the café since I forgot to take a picture. Vintage enamelware and the inedible curly parsley garnish brings me back to Chernobyl. The only thing missing is a pack of dogs barking outside. The New York City pups don't cut it.

I woke up the next morning feeling refreshed and ready for more adventures. It was time to visit Pripyat, the abandoned city whose shadow loomed over the zone.

PRIPYAT

51°38'83.81", 30°07'69.32" – 51.407161, 30.054998

I STOOD
IN EMPTY
APARTMENTS
THAT USED
TO BE HOME.

You are now entering the city of Pripyat.
I wish US cities had bold signs like this.

The first thing I noticed about the sign was its
relatively good condition. It looked like I was
just entering another city on my tour of Ukraine.
Then, the reality sank in. Nobody was living in
Pripyat and probably nobody ever would again.
There were no animals thanks to the winter season,
no birds crying overhead, no squirrels scurrying
through the underbrush. I'd been expecting to
see this iconic sign, aware of all the infamy it
represented, but I was at a loss. The hospitality
of the people of Chernobyl stood in stark contrast
to the cold, quiet despair waiting for me ahead.
I felt like I was crossing a threshold. I was leaving
the relative warmth of Chernobyl for the mournful
repose of a phantom city.

Most parts of the zone, including Pripyat, have safe radiation levels aside from the hotspots. If you think it'd be cool to take a picture with a high number on the dosimeter (pictured), DO NOT go into the basement of a particular hospital in the area.

The highest number my dosimeter picked up was around 26 microsieverts per hour. In case you aren't a nerd like me and that measurement is meaningless, eating a banana is about 0.1 microsievert and a 12-hour flight is about 200 microsieverts. Honestly, I think I was exposed to more radiation during my flights to the zone rather than any of my adventures in it.

The largest radiation deposits are in living and formerly living materials like moss, bone, and vegetation. The radiation levels, like mercury levels in fish, get higher as you go up the food chain. The greatest plausible danger is ingesting a particle that emits alpha and beta radiation. Trust me, you don't want that stuff bouncing around inside your body. Or you could accidentally scrape your knee on the ground. Instead of a small cut, you could land yourself a free dose of chemo.

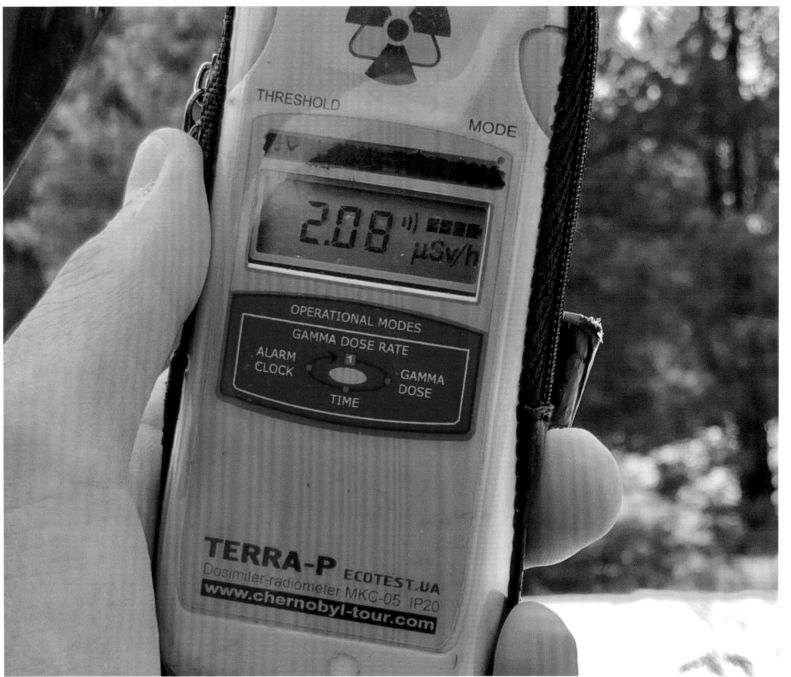

This is the guarded checkpoint to enter an abandoned residential area in Pripyat. The guard also had a fake gun that resembled an MG-42. I have no idea why, but I guessed it was mostly for show. There's minimal need for a weapon like that in a such a remote part of the zone. Maybe the tourists expect the scary guard to have a gun? Either way, all he did was operate the arm gate and smoke cigarettes.

CHECKPOINT

Looks nice enough to be part of a posh college campus, right? This is a school for young children, and, according to my guide, much nicer than others in the country. Only privileged kids went here.

Next Page

A hallway in the school. It looked like my old high school, and I was equal parts shocked and confused for a moment. I could feel the humid summer breeze blowing through the windows. Hear the students running to class as the late bell rang. But in Pripyat, everything was quiet. I felt like I'd stumbled into the silent version of a post-apocalyptic memory. I wondered, briefly, if anybody who'd attended this school ever came back.

I found the answer a little later on. I can't be sure, but I think the red message was written by a former student. It says, roughly, "It's our life, pain, loss...2016."

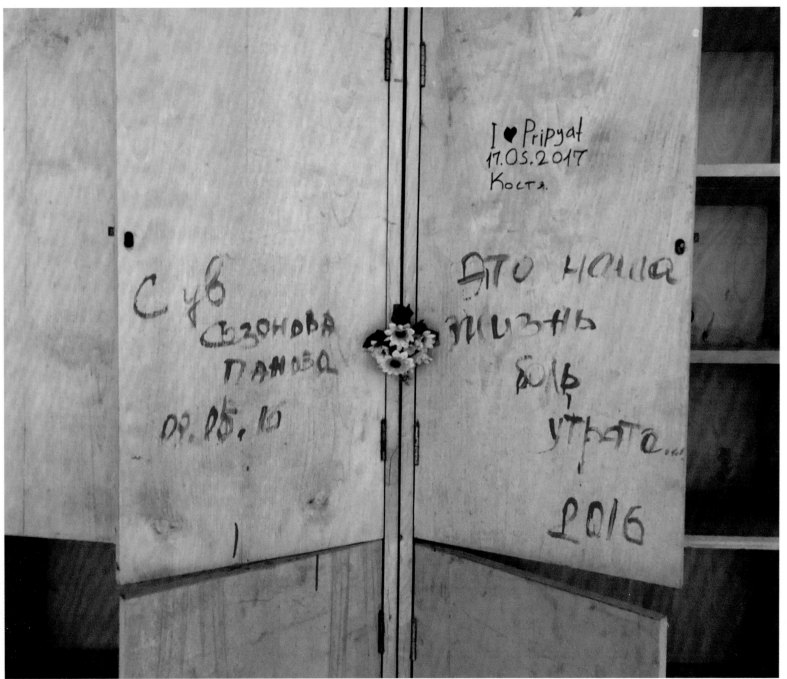

ONE OF THE WORST FEELINGS
I HAD ON THE ENTIRE TRIP WAS
STEPPING ON THESE BOOKS.

THE DILAPIDATED SCHOOL WAS
LITTERED WITH THEM, FROM THE
CLASSROOMS TO THE HALLWAYS.

THEY REMINDED ME OF ALL THE
CHILDHOODS DISRUPTED BY THE
ACCIDENT. CHILDREN SHOULDN'T
HAVE TO GO THROUGH
MASS EVACUATIONS.

A cash register in the cafeteria. I left a one-hryvnia note with my name on it in a register. If you ever visit and find it, could you please take a photo and email me?

Next Page

I guess this is what teachers used before PowerPoint was invented. Where's the button to add a star wipe?

Looks morbid, but gas masks have an interesting history in the zone. Almost none of these were used as intended. Instead, they were picked clean by looters after the fact since the filters contained valuable metals. The residents of Chernobyl were prepared for the end of the world via nuclear attack by the west, but, ironically, their world was destroyed by their own government.

...

THE KIDS IN THIS SCHOOL
EVACUATED SO QUICKLY THEY HAD
TO LEAVE THEIR ART PROJECTS
BEHIND. THESE REMINDED ME OF
ALL THE ARTS AND CRAFTS I DID
WHEN I WAS THEIR AGE.
BEFORE MY TRIP, I NEVER THOUGHT
IT WAS A PRIVILEGE TO BE ABLE
TO TAKE HOME MY MACARONI
PICTURES AND FINGER PAINTINGS.
AN ENTIRE GENERATION WAS
ROBBED OF THAT CHOICE.

I found a lot of propaganda in the school. Here's one I thought was funny—a collage explaining America to Soviet children. The authorities were obviously trying to convince these kids that America was full of warmongering capitalists. Note the big guns, mustaches, and cowboy hats. Not very subtle, but then again Soviet propaganda was never known for a nuanced view on the issues.

51°40′61.99″, 30°04′87.11″

...

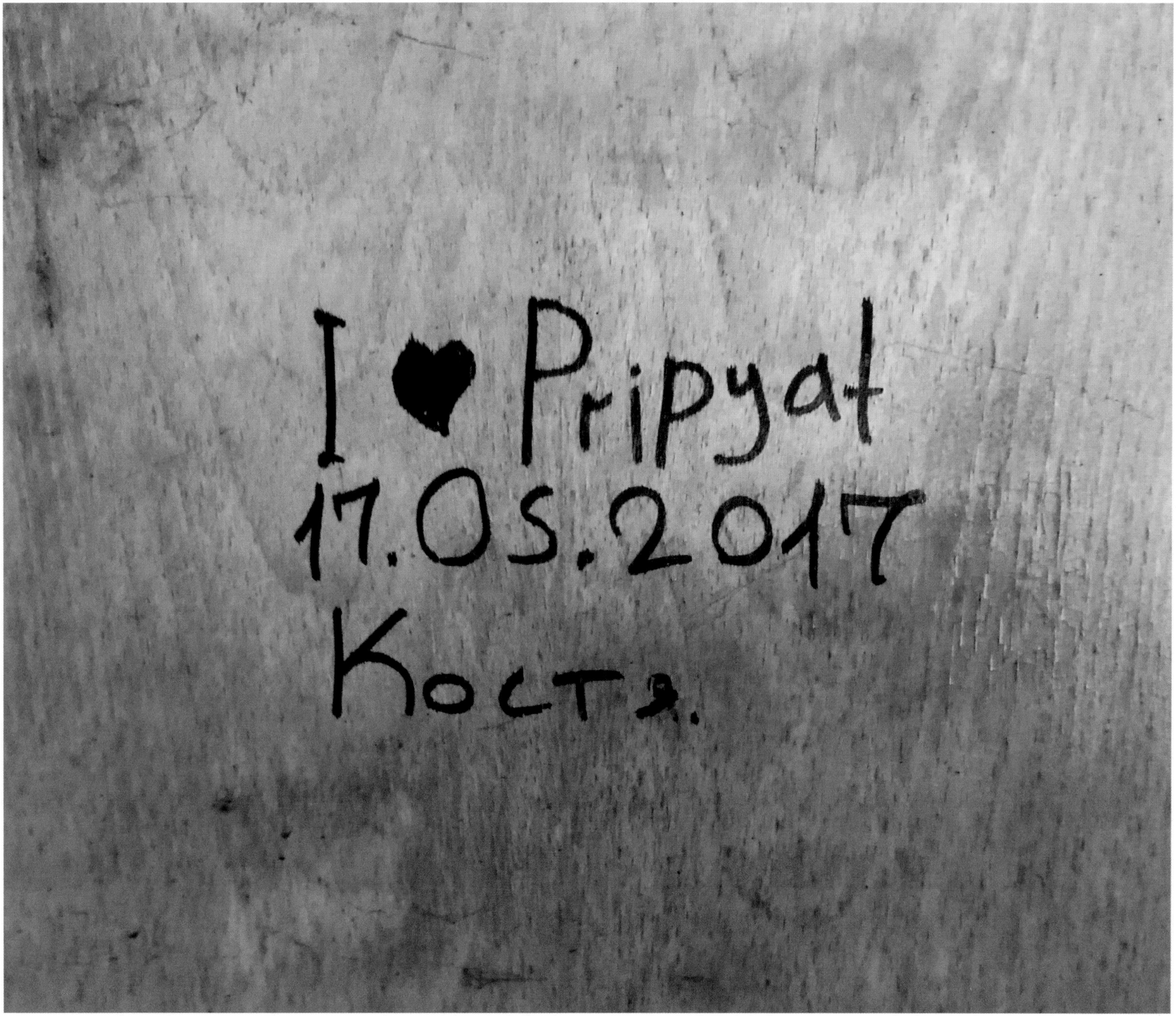
I ♥ Pripyat
17.05.2017
Костя.

Пионерская
ПРАВДА

BUT THERE'S A DISTANCE TO THE TRAGEDY

I found this newspaper in the school. It was dated
three days before the reactor meltdown. Surprisingly,
the articles covered economic reform and other
complicated issues. Elementary school kids were
expected to read this stuff. Can you imagine a
third grader sitting still long enough to learn about
trade deficits and collective farming?

Next Page
The iconic Pripyat landmark, the Azure Swimming Pool.
This place was actually open after the disaster for
liquidators to use. However, it was officially closed
in 1998 after bad weather broke the surrounding
windows and radioactive material swept inside.

SCHOOLS IN PRIPYAT

SWIMMING POOL

THIS GHOSTLY
CITY WILL
FOREVER BE
A SOBERING
REMINDER.

Did I just hear a Scottish man mumbling about how 50,000 people used to live here? This was taken on top of a 15-floor residential building. As I walked up, I poked inside some apartments. They were mostly empty. Everything had been looted except for the heavy stuff like bathtubs and stoves. What shook me the most was how the apartments looked similar to ones I'd seen earlier in other parts of Ukraine. Those, of course, were full of furniture and people while the Pripyat versions were hollow shells. Only traces of their previous residents survived. Some still had curtains hanging next to the windows. I was acutely aware a Pripyat citizen picked out those specific curtains and hung them with their own two hands.

Some apartments were locked. I wanted to explore every last one, but I didn't have enough time. Part of me is glad I never found out what's on the other side of those locked doors. I'll be thinking about the mystery of those forbidden apartments for a long time. Unfortunately, I did find areas that had been disturbed by tourists. The zone should be treated like a museum: look all you want, but don't touch. It's wrong to rearrange artifacts for your "perfect" Instagram photo. These are peoples' belongings, not props for your enjoyment.

Once I reached the roof, the silence was deafening. I'd never felt more alone in my entire life. And yet, there was beauty in the stillness, like the world stopped turning on April 26th, 1986. Did you know power was fed to Pripyat up to the year 2000? I wish I could've seen the roads light up under the automatic street lights. Maybe the empty apartments would've lit up too, as if the city kept living despite every resident evacuating, as if nothing had changed.

TOP OF BUILDING VIEW

MAYBE THE EMPTY
APARTMENTS WOULD'VE
LIT UP TOO, AS IF THE
CITY KEPT LIVING
DESPITE EVERY RESIDENT
EVACUATING, AS IF
NOTHING HAD CHANGED.

...

Seeing the Chernobyl power plant must've filled
the residents here with pride. Pride in their city,
their country, and maybe even in humanity itself.
Pripyat was the crown jewel of this area. It was
Soviet propaganda made real. The people who
lived here had good jobs, nice houses, and some
of the best food and alcohol available in the nation.
They sent their children to upscale schools while
doing important work in the power plant alongside
friends and neighbors. The same laws of physics
that could've ended the world had literally been
turned into fuel for mankind's march forward.
There was no reason to be anything but optimistic
about the future in Pripyat.

Sadly, a preventable accident at the reactor ended
up stigmatizing nuclear power forever. As someone
who works in R&D, visiting Pripyat helped me realize
the importance of taking responsibility for the
awesome technology we create. This ghostly city
will forever be a sobering reminder, a breathless
memorial to what happens when we don't use our
creations safely.

Remember the fake bus stop built for the Duga staff and the hidden military town? This is what the receiver looked like from Pripyat. Imagine being a resident here, seeing that metal beast, and having no idea what it was for. I wonder if they ever got even a little curious. I'm sure the plan made sense when the officials were discussing it over tea and cigarettes, but that thing is hard to hide. Maybe they assumed people would eventually get used to it and forget it was there? Maybe they hid it in plain sight.

IMAGINE BEING
A RESIDENT HERE,
SEEING THAT
METAL BEAST,
AND HAVING
NO IDEA WHAT IT
WAS FOR.

Who's up for a carnival ride? I wouldn't recommend it. One of the carriages in the bottom center had a piece of radioactive material inside. The liquidators used this area as a helicopter landing zone, so the rotors probably blew it into the ferris wheel. That being said, the carnival had been used a couple times before the official May 1st opening. That's a small window before the accident on April 26th, but at least somebody got to enjoy the rides. I now realize that this carnival is emblematic of the Soviet—a reminder of what could've been, what never was, what never will be.

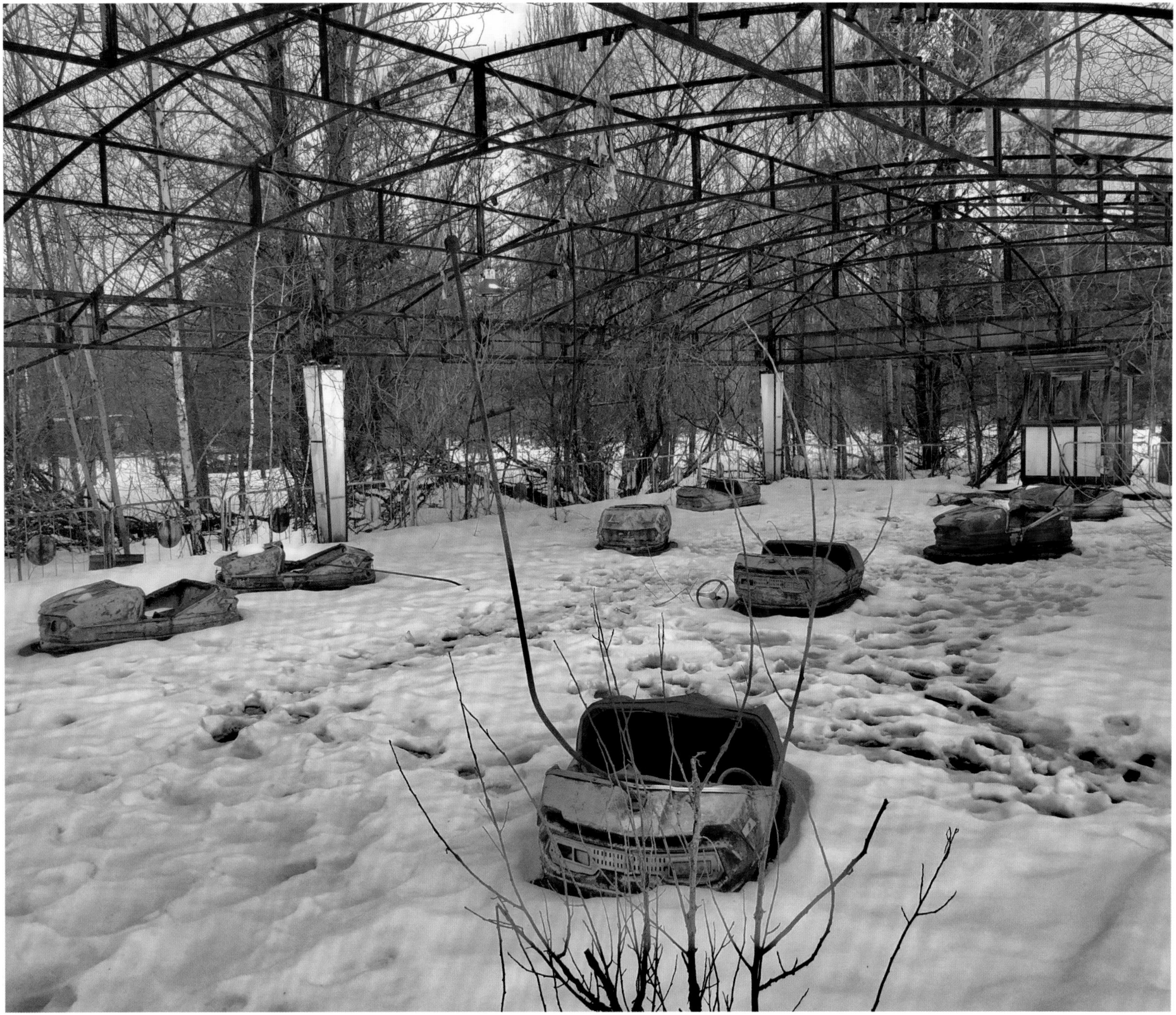

51°24'29.9", 30°03'22.1"

CARNIVAL

The sign says "Polissya Hotel." As one of the bigger buildings in Pripyat, the liquidators turned the hotel into an impromptu command center during cleanup efforts. They probably weren't the guests the hotel owners were expecting. If you want a laugh, look up the hotel online. The reviews are decent considering its proximity to the worst nuclear disaster in human history.

On a slightly related note, I'm pretty sure this is the building where Price and MacMillan sniped Zakhaev in Call of Duty 4.

Like I said earlier, Pripyat was a prestigious town.
It was described to me as the Silicon Valley of
the Soviet Union. Smart people worked here and
were well-compensated financially and socially.
The supermarket in Pripyat, for example, was
stocked with some items that weren't available
even in Moscow. In fact, it was one of the few
places in the nation rumored to carry Chanel No. 5.
As you can see, the hanging blue banners were
impossibly vibrant. It was surreal seeing brightly
colored signs in such dilapidated conditions.
Beauty can hide in the most unassuming places.

There was a bulletin board next to the grocery
store that had been used for local news. When I
was there, I found stalkers had covered the boards
with laminated biographies of people who died
because of the incident. I also found a freshly
painted playground. What drives stalkers to care
for a place forsaken by the rest of the world?
Is it some sense of ownership or stewardship?
Is it their way of reclaiming what was lost?
I'm still trying to answer this myself.

IN FACT,
IT WAS ONE OF
THE FEW PLACES IN
THE NATION
RUMORED TO CARRY
CHANEL NO. 5.

These were taken inside a Pripyat post office. Letters were sorted in the area in the left picture. The other space looks like it has a bunch of closets, but they're actually phone booths. Since many people in the Soviet Union didn't own phones, these rooms were an important way of keeping in touch with friends and family. I wonder what kinds of conversations happened in here.
Cousins catching up on family gossip? Anastasia talking to her boyfriend, Dima, while twirling her hair around her finger?

POST OFFICE AND TELEPHONE VIEW

I'm not sure if these books had been arranged
by a tourist or stalker, or simply left like this
since the disaster. It looks almost normal, right?
I half-expected to hear the pitter-patter of
children coming down the hallway.

This is School No. 1. It's situated in the central town square near the grocery store. The entrance collapsed some time ago. Also, the snow was melting, so I was hesitant to enter because water damage might've made the remaining structure unstable. However, I still went inside, and I'm glad I did.

These posters were the newest propaganda in Pripyat at the time. The colors were so vibrant compared to other pre-disaster printed material I'd seen, except for the banners in the supermarket.

БЕССМЕРТЕН
ТВОИ
ПОДВИГ
СОЛДАТ

PEOPLE BECAME
TOOLS THAT DAY,
AND SOME PAID
A HUGE PRICE.

This was inside Pripyat Café. The sign on the building literally says "Pripyat." What a great name for a
restaurant, it cuts straight to the point. This place is
near the water, so it must've been nice to visit back
in the day. I also found what looked like some kind
of mosaic and, on the ground near it, stacks of thin,
colored glass sandwiched together.

These pictures are important because they prove
there was still color in the zone. It wasn't drab and
grey as it's portrayed in movies and video games.
I found vibrant art tucked away inside an unassuming
grey building, sure, but that proved how the zone
was filled with hidden beauty.

A REMINDER OF
WHAT COULD'VE BEEN,
WHAT NEVER WAS,
WHAT NEVER WILL BE.

I took these pictures at a hospital officially known
as Medical unit No. 126 (МедСанЧастина № 126).
I found handwritten notes in what looked like a
maternity ward, probably left behind by a nurse,
only to be rearranged by someone for their
Instagram post.

I was told all women who were pregnant around the
time of the disaster were forced to get abortions.
An entire generation was wiped out before they
were born. Think about all the stories cut short.

ENDING

...

And finally, the Chernobyl power plant. My last stop was the place where all this started. I couldn't believe how many lives were affected by Reactor No. 4. Entire cities, towns, and villages were emptied. An entire generation forced into exile. An entire country catapulted into the national spotlight. The disaster I'd thought I knew so well had become human for me. My trip answered old questions and raised new ones I'm not sure I'll ever figure out. My world got bigger thanks to exploring the zone in all its sadness and warmth and beauty. I'll never forget my time there.

CLOSING NOTE

At first, I thought it'd be cool to visit the zone because of how it has captivated the public in news and fiction. However, what I thought would be a breezy and fun vacation turned into an extremely meaningful experience. It was hard to empathize from photographs of the disaster. Yes, the images of the blown reactor and fleeing families were shocking, but there's a distance to the tragedy when seen that way. The incident still felt exotic, removed, something that happened in a far away land with no direct consequence on my life. Frankly, the pictures were too similar to other disaster and war photos. We get numb to it after a while.

Then, I found childrens' homework strewn about an abandoned school. I stood in empty apartments that used to be home for some family. I found traces of life that made the people in those photographs real. My trip helped me understand the gravity of the accident, how so many people just like me were thrown into chaos on a random Saturday. I hope this book gave you a new perspective on those lives in and around the zone.

Thanks for reading.

APPENDIX

ENTERING DUGA-1 RADAR INSTALLATION

This fire station was the first building I explored after the villages. Did you know that during the cleanup, the liquidators sent in remote-controlled robots? Yeah, just like WALL-E. Unfortunately, the effort failed because of the tremendous amount of radiation. Gamma ray background radiation near the reactor reached about 28 sieverts per hour (a lot) and up to 98 per hour in some areas (a hell of a lot). Needless to say, most of the robots didn't stand a chance. Even a special robot from West Germany got fried, despite being designed to survive a rocket launch and work on the moon.

There was a simple and dangerous solution—send humans in. A special group of liquidators braved the disaster area with lead plates and rubber suits to mitigate the radioactivity. The official term for these workers was "bio-robots." People became tools that day, and some paid a huge price.

CRUMBS

You're still here? I hate to break it to you, but the book is over.
Well, kind of. I took a ton of great photos, mostly for myself,
but couldn't find a way to weave them into the book.
Take a look and enjoy!

WE LIVE *in the* SOVIET UNION

HOPE

WRITING

Hyun Kyu Seo
Neil Floyd

PHOTOGRAPHS

Hyun Kyu Seo

ARTWORK

Hyun Kyu Seo
Ho Joung Seo
Colin Laflin

DESIGN

Hyun Kyu Seo
Matthew Higgins

SPECIAL THANKS

Alex Grover
Alexander Vincente
Julia Hripunova
Michael Weldon

HYUN KYU SEO

I was born in South Korea, but my heart is probably somewhere in Eastern Europe. My love affair with the region started back in high school when I took Russian for my language requirement. After I played the video game *S.T.A.L.K.E.R.: Shadow of Chernobyl,* I was fascinated by the nuclear disaster's tragic history and had to learn as much as I could about it. I decided I was going to see the zone for myself one day.

My other interests include all things tech—I hold patents in artificial intelligence, robotics, cyber-security, and quantum computing. More importantly, I hacked through my first firewall in middle school so I could mess around on Myspace and YouTube. If any of my old teachers are reading this, I'm sorry. A little.

I live in Austin and work at IBM Research. I've hosted popular workshops at SXSW and have been interviewed by publications such as *The Daily Dot* and *USA Today*.